Dave,

With this gi... ♡

With this gift my best wishes
for your future happiness.

Miss Kepplinger—

SOLILOQUIES
AND SPEECHES
FROM THE PLAYS
OF WILLIAM
SHAKESPEARE

ILLUSTRATED BY JEFF HILL FOR
THE PETER PAUPER PRESS
Mount Vernon • New York

SHAKESPEARE:
SOLILOQUIES
AND SPEECHES

. . .

Where should this music be? I' the air, or the earth?
It sounds no more. And sure it waits upon
Some god o' the island. Sitting on a bank,
Weeping again the King my father's wreck,
This music crept by me upon the waters,
Allaying both their fury and my passion
With its sweet air. Thence I have followed it,
Or it hath drawn me rather — but 'tis gone.
No, it begins again.

The Tempest I · 2

THESEUS:

More strange than true. I never may believe
These antique fables, nor these fairy toys.
Lovers and madmen have such seething brains,
Such shaping fantasies, that apprehend
More than cool reason ever comprehends.
The lunatic, the lover, and the poet
Are of imagination all compact.
One sees more devils than vast hell can hold;
That is the madman. The lover, all as frantic,
Sees Helen's beauty in a brow of Egypt.
The poet's eye, in a fine frenzy rolling,
Doth glance from heaven to earth, from earth to
   heaven.
And as imagination bodies forth
The forms of things unknown, the poet's pen
Turns them to shapes, and gives to airy nothing
A local habitation, and a name.
Such tricks hath strong imagination,
That if it would but apprehend some joy,
It comprehends some bringer of that joy.
Or in the night, imagining some fear,
How easy is a bush supposed a bear!

A Midsummer Night's Dream V · 1

5

SHYLOCK:

Signior Antonio, many a time and oft
In the Rialto you have rated me
About my moneys and my usances.
Still have I borne it with a patient shrug,
For sufferance is the badge of all our tribe.
You call me misbeliever, cut-throat dog,
And spit upon my Jewish gaberdine,
And all for use of that which is mine own.
Well then, it now appears you need my help.
Go to then, you come to me, and you say,
Shylock, we would have moneys — you say so;
You that did void your rheum upon my beard,
And foot me as you spurn a stranger cur
Over your threshold — moneys is your suit.
What should I say to you? Should I not say,
Hath a dog money? Is it possible
A cur can lend three thousand ducats? Or
Shall I bend low, and in a bondman's key
With bated breath, and whispering humbleness,
Say this —
Fair sir, you spit on me on Wednesday last,
You spurned me such a day, another time
You called me dog; and for these courtesies
I'll lend you thus much moneys?

The Merchant of Venice I · 3

6

PORTIA:

The quality of mercy is not strained,
It droppeth as the gentle rain from heaven
Upon the place beneath. It is twice blessed —
It blesseth him that gives, and him that takes.
'Tis mightiest in the mightiest, it becomes
The thronèd monarch better than his crown.
His sceptre shows the force of temporal power,
The attribute to awe and majesty,
Wherein doth sit the dread and fear of kings.
But mercy is above this sceptred sway,
It is enthronèd in the hearts of kings,
It is an attribute to God himself;
And earthly power doth then show likest God's
When mercy seasons justice. Therefore Jew,
Though justice be thy plea, consider this,
That in the course of justice, none of us
Should see salvation. We do pray for mercy,
And that same prayer doth teach us all to render
The deeds of mercy. I have spoke thus much
To mitigate the justice of thy plea,
Which if thou follow, this strict court of Venice
Must needs give sentence 'gainst the merchant
   there.

The Merchant of Venice IV · 1

DUKE SENIOR:

Now my co-mates and brothers in exile,
Hath not old custom made this life more sweet
Than that of painted pomp? Are not these woods
More free from peril than the envious court?
Here feel we not the penalty of Adam,
The seasons' difference, as the icy fang
And churlish chiding of the winter's wind,
Which when it bites and blows upon my body
Even till I shrink with cold, I smile, and say
This is no flattery; these are counsellors
That feelingly persuade me what I am.
Sweet are the uses of adversity,
Which, like the toad ugly and venomous,
Wears yet a precious jewel in his head.
And this our life, exempt from public haunt,
Finds tongues in trees, books in the running
    brooks,
Sermons in stones, and good in every thing.

As You Like It   II · 1

JAQUES:

                    All the world's a stage,
And all the men and women merely players.
They have their exits and their entrances,
And one man in his time plays many parts,

His acts being seven ages. At first the infant,
Mewling, and puking in the nurse's arms.
Then the whining schoolboy with his satchel
And shining morning face, creeping like snail
Unwillingly to school. And then the lover,
Sighing like furnace, with a woeful ballad
Made to his mistress' eyebrow. Then, a soldier,
Full of strange oaths, and bearded like the pard,
Jealous in honour, sudden and quick in quarrel,
Seeking the bubble reputation
Even in the cannon's mouth. And then, the
    justice,
In fair round belly, with good capon lined,
With eyes severe, and beard of formal cut,
Full of wise saws and modern instances,
And so he plays his part. The sixth age shifts
Into the lean and slippered pantaloon,
With spectacles on nose, and pouch on side,
His youthful hose well saved, a world too wide
For his shrunk shank, and his big manly voice,
Turning again toward childish treble pipes
And whistles in his sound. Last scene of all,
That ends this strange eventful history,
Is second childishness and mere oblivion,
Sans teeth, sans eyes, sans taste, sans every thing.

As You Like It II · 7

10

BASTARD:

Ha majesty! How high thy glory towers,
When the rich blood of kings is set on fire.
O now doth Death line his dead chaps with steel;
The swords of soldiers are his teeth, his fangs,
And now he feasts, mousing the flesh of men,
In undetermined differences of kings.
Why stand these royal fronts amazèd thus?
Cry havoc Kings, back to the stainèd field,
You equal potents, fiery kindled spirits!
Then let confusion of one part confirm
The other's peace; till then, blows, blood, and
    death!

King John II · 1

CONSTANCE:

Thou art not holy to belie me so,
I am not mad. This hair I tear is mine,
My name is Constance, I was Geffrey's wife,
Young Arthur is my son, and he is lost.

. . .

Grief fills the room up of my absent child,
Lies in his bed, walks up and down with me,
Puts on his pretty looks, repeats his words,
Remembers me of all his gracious parts,
Stuffs out his vacant garments with his form;

11

Then, have I reason to be fond of grief?
Fare you well; had you such a loss as I,
I could give better comfort than you do.
I will not keep this form upon my head,
When there is such disorder in my wit.
O lord, my boy, my Arthur, my fair son,
My life, my joy, my food, my all the world!
My widow-comfort, and my sorrows' cure!

King John   III · 4

BASTARD: [*as* HUBERT *takes body up*]

I am amazed methinks, and lose my way
Among the thorns and dangers of this world.
How easy dost thou take all England up!
From forth this morsel of dead royalty,
The life, the right, and truth of all this realm
Is fled to heaven; and England now is left
To tug and scamble, and to part by th' teeth
The unowed interest of proud swelling state.
Now for the bare-picked bone of majesty
Doth dogged war bristle his angry crest,
And snarleth in the gentle eyes of peace.

King John   IV · 3

PRINCE HENRY:

O vanity of sickness; fierce extremes
In their continuance will not feel themselves.

Death, having preyed upon the outward parts,
Leaves them unusable, and his siege is now
Against the mind, the which he pricks and
    wounds
With many legions of strange fantasies,
Which in their throng and press to that last hold,
Confound themselves. 'Tis strange that death
    should sing.
I am the cygnet to this pale faint swan,
Who chants a doleful hymn to his own death,
And from the organ-pipe of frailty sings
His soul and body to their lasting rest.

      • • •

       How fares your Majesty?

JOHN:

Poisonèd, ill fare — dead, forsook, cast off,
And none of you will bid the winter come
To thrust his icy fingers in my maw;
Nor let my kingdom's rivers take their course
Through my burnt bosom; nor entreat the north
To make his bleak winds kiss my parchèd lips,
And comfort me with cold. I do not ask you
    much,
I beg cold comfort; and you are so strait
And so ingrateful, you deny me that.

              King John V · 7

14

GAUNT:

This royal throne of kings, this sceptred isle,
This earth of majesty, this seat of Mars,
This other Eden, demi-Paradise,
This fortress built by Nature for herself
Against infection and the hand of war,
This happy breed of men, this little world,
This precious stone set in the silver sea,
Which serves it in the office of a wall,
Or as a moat defensive to a house,
Against the envy of less happier lands;
This blessèd plot, this earth, this realm, this
    England,
This nurse, this teeming womb of royal kings,
Feared by their breed, and famous by their birth,
Renownèd for their deeds as far from home,
For Christian service, and true chivalry,
As is the sepulchre in stubborn Jewry,
Of the world's ransom, blessèd Mary's Son.
This land of such dear souls, this dear dear land,
Dear for her reputation through the world,
Is now leased out — I die pronouncing it —
Like to a tenement or pelting farm.
England bound in with the triumphant sea,
Whose rocky shore beats back the envious siege
Of watery Neptune, is now bound in with shame,

With inky blots, and rotten parchment bonds.
That England that was wont to conquer others,
Hath made a shameful conquest of itself.

King Richard the Second II · 1

RICHARD:

No matter where, of comfort no man speak.
Let's talk of graves, of worms, and epitaphs,
Make dust our paper, and with rainy eyes,
Write sorrow on the bosom of the earth.
Let's choose executors and talk of wills.
And yet not so, for what can we bequeath,
Save our deposèd bodies to the ground?
Our lands, our lives, and all are Bolingbroke's,
And nothing can we call our own, but death;
And that small model of the barren earth,
Which serves as paste, and cover to our bones.
For God's sake let us sit upon the ground,
And tell sad stories of the death of kings,
How some have been deposed, some slain in war,
Some haunted by the ghosts they have deposed,
Some poisoned by their wives, some sleeping
    killed,
All murdered. For within the hollow crown
That rounds the mortal temples of a king

Keeps Death his court, and there the antic sits,
Scoffing his state and grinning at his pomp,
Allowing him a breath, a little scene,
To monarchize, be feared, and kill with looks,
Infusing him with self and vain conceit,
As if this flesh which walls about our life,
Were brass impregnable; and humoured thus,
Comes at the last and with a little pin
Bores through his castle wall, and farewell king!
Cover your heads, and mock not flesh and blood,
With solemn reverence; throw away respect,
Tradition, form, and ceremonious duty,
For you have but mistook me all this while.
I live with bread like you, feel want,
Taste grief, need friends; subjected thus,
How can you say to me, I am a King?

King Richard the Second III · 2

KING HENRY:

How many thousand of my poorest subjects
Are at this hour asleep! O sleep, o gentle sleep,
Nature's soft nurse, how have I frighted thee,
That thou no more wilt weigh my eyelids down,
And steep my senses in forgetfulness?
Why rather, sleep, liest thou in smoky cribs,

Upon uneasy pallets stretching thee,
And hushed with buzzing night-flies to thy
        slumber,
Than in the perfumed chambers of the great,
Under the canopies of costly state,
And lulled with sound of sweetest melody?
O thou dull god, why li'st thou with the vile
In loathsome beds, and leav'st the kingly couch
A watch-case, or a common 'larum-bell?
Wilt thou upon the high and giddy mast
Seal up the ship-boy's eyes, and rock his brains
In cradle of the rude imperious surge,
And in the visitation of the winds,
Who take the ruffian billows by the top,
Curling their monstrous heads, and hanging
        them
With deafing clamour in the slippery clouds,
That with the hurly death itself awakes?
Canst thou, o partial sleep, give thy repose
To the wet seas' son in an hour so rude,
And in the calmest and most stillest night,
With all appliances and means to boot,
Deny it to a king? Then, happy low, lie down,
Uneasy lies the head that wears a crown.

King Henry the Fourth: Part Two   III · 1

19

PRINCE HENRY:

I never thought to hear you speak again.

KING HENRY:

Thy wish was father, Harry, to that thought.
I stay too long by thee, I weary thee.
Dost thou so hunger for mine empty chair,
That thou wilt needs invest thee with my honours,
Before thy hour be ripe? O foolish youth,
Thou seek'st the greatness that will overwhelm
    thee.
Stay but a little, for my cloud of dignity
Is held from falling with so weak a wind
That it will quickly drop; my day is dim.
Thou hast stol'n that which after some few hours
Were thine without offence, and at my death
Thou hast sealed up my expectation.
Thy life did manifest thou loved'st me not,
And thou wilt have me die assured of it.
Thou hid'st a thousand daggers in thy thoughts,
Which thou hast whetted on thy stony heart,
To stab at half an hour of my life.
What, canst thou not forbear me half an hour?
Then, get thee gone, and dig my grave thyself,
And bid the merry bells ring to thine ear,
That thou art crowned, not that I am dead.
Let all the tears that should bedew my hearse

Be drops of balm, to sanctify thy head.
Only compound me with forgotten dust,
Give that which gave thee life unto the worms,
Pluck down my officers, break my decrees,
For now a time is come to mock at form.
Harry the Fifth is crowned. Up vanity!
Down royal state! All you sage counsellors,
    hence,
And to the English Court assemble now
From every region, apes of idleness!
Now, neighbour confines, purge you of your scum.
Have you a ruffian that will swear, drink, dance,
Revel the night, rob, murder, and commit
The oldest sins the newest kind of ways?
Be happy, he will trouble you no more.
England shall double gild his treble guilt,
England shall give him office, honour, might;
For the Fifth Harry from curbed licence plucks
The muzzle of restraint, and the wild dog
Shall flesh his tooth on every innocent.
O my poor kingdom, sick with civil blows!
When that my care could not withhold thy riots,
What wilt thou do when riot is thy care?
O thou wilt be a wilderness again,
Peopled with wolves, thy old inhabitants!

King Henry the Fourth: Part Two IV · 5

22

HENRY:

Once more unto the breach, dear friends,
    once more;
Or close the wall up with our English dead.
In peace, there's nothing so becomes a man,
As modest stillness, and humility.
But when the blast of war blows in our ears,
Then imitate the action of the tiger;
Stiffen the sinews, summon up the blood,
Disguise fair nature with hard-favoured rage.
Then lend the eye a terrible aspect;
Let it pry through the portage of the head,
Like the brass cannon; let the brow o'erwhelm it,
As fearfully as doth a gallèd rock
O'erhang and jutty his confounded base,
Swilled with the wild and wasteful ocean.
Now set the teeth, and stretch the nostril wide,
Hold hard the breath, and bend up every spirit
To his full height. On, on, you noblest English,
Whose blood is fet from fathers of war-proof;
Fathers, that like so many Alexanders,
Have in these parts from morn till even fought,
And sheathed their swords for lack of argument.
Dishonour not your mothers; now attest,
That those whom you called fathers did beget you.

            King Henry the Fifth III · 1

HENRY:

If we are marked to die, we are enow
To do our country loss; and if to live,
The fewer men, the greater share of honour.
God's will, I pray thee wish not one man more.
By Jove, I am not covetous for gold,
Nor care I who doth feed upon my cost.
It yearns me not if men my garments wear;
Such outward things dwell not in my desires.
But if it be a sin to covet honour,
I am the most offending soul alive.
No faith, my coz, wish not a man from England.
God's peace, I would not lose so great an honour,
As one man more methinks would share from
     me,
For the best hope I have. O, do not wish one
     more.
Rather proclaim it, Westmorland, through my
     host,
That he which hath no stomach to this fight,
Let him depart; his passport shall be made,
And crowns for convoy put into his purse.
We would not die in that man's company,
That fears his fellowship to die with us.

                    King Henry the Fifth IV · 3

24

RICHARD:

Now is the winter of our discontent
Made glorious summer by this sun of York;
And all the clouds that loured upon our house
In the deep bosom of the ocean burièd.
Now are our brows bound with victorious wreaths,
Our bruisèd arms hung up for monuments,
Our stern alarums changed to merry meetings,
Our dreadful marches to delightful measures.
Grim-visaged war hath smoothed his wrinkled
     front;
And now, instead of mounting barbèd steeds,
To fright the souls of fearful adversaries,
He capers nimbly in a lady's chamber,
To the lascivious pleasing of a lute.
But I, that am not shaped for sportive tricks,
Nor made to court an amorous looking-glass;
I, that am rudely stamped, and want love's majesty,
To strut before a wanton ambling nymph;
I, that am curtailèd of this fair proportion,
Cheated of feature by dissembling nature,
Deformed, unfinished, sent before my time
Into this breathing world, scarce half made up,
And that so lamely and unfashionable
That dogs bark at me as I halt by them —
Why I, in this weak piping time of peace,

Have no delight to pass away the time,
Unless to see my shadow in the sun,
And descant on mine own deformity.
And therefore, since I cannot prove a lover,
To entertain these fair well-spoken days,
I am determinèd to prove a villain,
And hate the idle pleasures of these days.

King Richard the Third I · 1

CORIOLANUS:

You common cry of curs, whose breath I hate
As reek a th' rotten fens, whose loves I prize
As the dead carcasses of unburied men,
That do corrupt my air; I banish you,
And here remain with your uncertainty.
Let every feeble rumour shake your hearts.
Your enemies with nodding of their plumes
Fan you into despair. Have the power still
To banish your defenders, till at length

. . .

Still your own foes, deliver you, as most
Abated captives, to some nation
That won you without blows. Despising
For you the city, thus I turn my back.
There is a world elsewhere.

Coriolanus III · 3

WOLSEY:

So farewell — to the little good you bear me.
Farewell? A long farewell to all my greatness.
This is the state of man: to-day he puts forth
The tender leaves of hope; to-morrow blossoms,
And bears his blushing honours thick upon him;
The third day comes a frost, a killing frost,
And when he thinks, good easy man, full surely
His greatness is a-ripening, nips his root,
And then he falls as I do. I have ventured
Like little wanton boys that swim on bladders,
This many summers in a sea of glory,
But far beyond my depth. My high-blown pride
At length broke under me, and now has left me,
Weary, and old with service, to the mercy
Of a rude stream, that must for ever hide me.
Vain pomp, and glory of this world, I hate ye;
I feel my heart new opened. O how wretched
Is that poor man that hangs on princes' favours!
There is betwixt that smile we would aspire to,
That sweet aspect of princes, and their ruin,
More pangs and fears than wars or women have;
And when he falls, he falls like Lucifer,
Never to hope again.

King Henry the Eighth III · 2

27

ROMEO:

O she doth teach the torches to burn bright.
It seems she hangs upon the cheek of night
As a rich jewel in an Ethiop's ear
Beauty too rich for use, for earth too dear.
So shows a snowy dove trooping with crows,
As yonder lady o'er her fellows shows.

·   ·   ·

Did my heart love till now? Forswear it sight,
For I ne'er saw true beauty till this night.

Romeo and Juliet I · 5

ROMEO:

But soft, what light through yonder window
        breaks?
It is the East, and Juliet is the sun.
Arise fair sun and kill the envious moon,
Who is already sick and pale with grief,
That thou her maid art far more fair than she.

Romeo and Juliet II · 2

ROMEO:

O my love, my wife!
Death that hath sucked the honey of thy breath,
Hath had no power yet upon thy beauty.
Thou art not conquered; beauty's ensign yet
Is crimson in thy lips and in thy cheeks,

28

And death's pale flag is not advancèd there.
Tybalt, liest thou there in thy bloody sheet?
O what more favour can I do to thee,
Than with that hand that cut thy youth in twain
To sunder his that was thine enemy?
Forgive me cousin. Ah dear Juliet,
Why art thou yet so fair? Shall I believe
That unsubstantial Death is amorous,
And that the lean abhorrèd monster keeps
Thee here in dark to be his paramour?
For fear of that, I still will stay with thee,
And never from this palace of dim night
Depart again. Here, here will I remain,
With worms that are thy chamber-maids. O here
Will I set up my everlasting rest;
And shake the yoke of inauspicious stars
From this world-wearied flesh. Eyes look your last.
Arms, take your last embrace. And lips, o you
The doors of breath, seal with a righteous kiss
A dateless bargain to engrossing death.
Come bitter conduct, come unsavoury guide,
Thou desperate pilot, now at once run on
The dashing rocks thy sea-sick weary bark.
Here's to my love! O true apothecary!
Thy drugs are quick. Thus with a kiss I die.

Romeo and Juliet V · 3

MARULLUS:

Wherefore rejoice? What conquest brings he home?
What tributaries follow him to Rome,
To grace in captive bonds his chariot wheels?
You blocks, you stones, you worse than senseless
    things!
O you hard hearts, you cruel men of Rome,
Knew you not Pompey? Many a time and oft
Have you climbed up to walls and battlements,
To towers and windows, yea, to chimney tops,
Your infants in your arms, and there have sat
The livelong day, with patient expectation,
To see great Pompey pass the streets of Rome.
And when you saw his chariot but appear,
Have you not made an universal shout,
That Tiber trembled underneath her banks,
To hear the replication of your sounds
Made in her concave shores?
And do you now put on your best attire?
And do you now cull out a holiday?
And do you now strew flowers in his way,
That comes in triumph over Pompey's blood?
Be gone! Run to your houses, fall upon your knees,
Pray to the gods to intermit the plague
That needs must light on this ingratitude.

Julius Cæsar I · 1

31

CASSIUS:

Why man, he doth bestride the narrow world
Like a Colossus, and we petty men
Walk under his huge legs, and peep about
To find ourselves dishonourable graves.
Men at some time are masters of their fates.
The fault, dear Brutus, is not in our stars,
But in ourselves, that we are underlings.
Brutus and Cæsar. What should be in that
    Cæsar?
Why should that name be sounded more than
    yours?
Write them together, yours is as fair a name.
Sound them, it doth become the mouth as well.
Weigh them, it is as heavy. Conjure with 'em,
Brutus will start a spirit as soon as Cæsar.
Now in the names of all the gods at once,
Upon what meat doth this our Cæsar feed,
That he is grown so great? Age, thou art shamed.
Rome, thou hast lost the breed of noble bloods.
When went there by an age, since the great flood,
But it was famed with more than with one man?
When could they say, till now, that talked of
    Rome,
That her wide walls encompassed but one man?

Julius Cæsar I · 2

32

ANTONY:

Friends, Romans, countrymen, lend me your
    ears.
I come to bury Cæsar, not to praise him.
The evil that men do, lives after them,
The good is oft interrèd with their bones;
So let it be with Cæsar. The noble Brutus
Hath told you Cæsar was ambitious;
If it were so, it was a grievous fault,
And grievously hath Cæsar answered it.
Here, under leave of Brutus, and the rest —
For Brutus is an honourable man,
So are they all, all honourable men —
Come I to speak in Cæsar's funeral.
He was my friend, faithful, and just to me;
But Brutus says, he was ambitious,
And Brutus is an honourable man.
He hath brought many captives home to Rome,
Whose ransoms did the general coffers fill.
Did this in Cæsar seem ambitious?
When that the poor have cried, Cæsar hath wept.
Ambition should be made of sterner stuff,
Yet Brutus says, he was ambitious;
And Brutus is an honourable man.
You all did see, that on the Lupercal
I thrice presented him a kingly crown,

Which he did thrice refuse. Was this ambition?
Yet Brutus says, he was ambitious;
And sure he is an honourable man.
I speak not to disprove what Brutus spoke,
But here I am, to speak what I do know;
You all did love him once, not without cause,
What cause withholds you then to mourn for
     him?
O judgment, thou art fled to brutish beasts,
And men have lost their reason. Bear with me;
My heart is in the coffin there with Cæsar,
And I must pause, till it come back to me.

          •   •   •

If you have tears, prepare to shed them now.
You all do know this mantle, I remember
The first time ever Cæsar put it on;
'Twas on a summer's evening in his tent,
That day he overcame the Nervii.
Look, in this place ran Cassius' dagger through.
See what a rent the envious Casca made.
Through this, the well-belovèd Brutus stabbed,
And as he plucked his cursèd steel away,
Mark how the blood of Cæsar followed it,
As rushing out of doors, to be resolved
If Brutus so unkindly knocked, or no;
For Brutus, as you know, was Cæsar's angel.

Judge, o you gods, how dearly Cæsar loved him.
This was the most unkindest cut of all;
For when the noble Cæsar saw him stab,
Ingratitude, more strong than traitors' arms,
Quite vanquished him. Then burst his mighty
    heart,
And in his mantle muffling up his face,
Even at the base of Pompey's statue,
Which all the while ran blood, great Cæsar fell.
O what a fall was there, my countrymen!
Then I, and you, and all of us fell down,
Whilst bloody treason flourished over us.
O now you weep, and I perceive you feel
The dint of pity. These are gracious drops.

Julius Cæsar   III · 2

ANTONY:

This was the noblest Roman of them all.
All the conspirators save only he
Did that they did, in envy of great Cæsar;
He only, in a general honest thought,
And common good to all, made one of them.
His life was gentle, and the elements
So mixed in him, that Nature might stand up,
And say to all the world, this was a man.

Julius Cæsar   V · 5

36

MACBETH:

Is this a dagger which I see before me,
The handle toward my hand? Come let me
    clutch thee.
I have thee not, and yet I see thee still.
Art thou not, fatal vision, sensible
To feeling as to sight? Or art thou but
A dagger of the mind, a false creation,
Proceeding from the heat-oppressed brain?
I see thee yet, in form as palpable
As this which now I draw.
Thou marshall'st me the way that I was going,
And such an instrument I was to use.
Mine eyes are made the fools o' th' other senses,
Or else worth all the rest. I see thee still;
And on thy blade and dudgeon gouts of blood,
Which was not so before. There's no such thing.
It is the bloody business which informs
Thus to mine eyes. Now o'er the one half-world
Nature seems dead, and wicked dreams abuse
The curtained sleep; witchcraft celebrates
Pale Hecate's offerings; and withered murder,
Alarumed by his sentinel the wolf,
Whose howl's his watch, thus with his stealthy
    pace,
With Tarquin's ravishing strides, towards his design

Moves like a ghost. Thou sure and firm-set earth,
Hear not my steps, which way they walk, for fear
Thy very stones prate of my whereabout,
And take the present horror from the time,
Which now suits with it. Whilst I threat, he lives.
Words to the heat of deeds too cold breath gives.

[*A bell rings within*]

I go, and it is done. The bell invites me.
Hear it not Duncan, for it is a knell
That summons thee to heaven, or to hell.

Macbeth II · 1

MACBETH:

Methought I heard a voice cry, sleep no more.
Macbeth does murder sleep, the innocent sleep,
Sleep that knits up the ravelled sleave of care,
The death of each day's life, sore labour's bath,
Balm of hurt minds, great nature's second
     course,
Chief nourisher in life's feast.

Macbeth II · 2

MACBETH:

We have scotched the snake, not killed it.
She'll close, and be herself, whilst our poor
     malice
Remains in danger of her former tooth.

39

But let the frame of things disjoint, both the
    worlds suffer,
Ere we will eat our meal in fear, and sleep
In the affliction of these terrible dreams
That shake us nightly. Better be with the dead,
Whom we, to gain our peace, have sent to peace,
Than on the torture of the mind to lie
In restless ecstasy. Duncan is in his grave.
After life's fitful fever he sleeps well,
Treason has done his worst; nor steel, nor poison,
Malice domestic, foreign levy, nothing,
Can touch him further.

                      Macbeth III · 2

MACBETH:

She should have died hereafter;
There would have been a time for such a word.
To-morrow, and to-morrow, and to-morrow,
Creeps in this petty pace from day to day,
To the last syllable of recorded time;
And all our yesterdays have lighted fools
The way to dusty death. Out, out, brief candle!
Life's but a walking shadow, a poor player,
That struts and frets his hour upon the stage,
And then is heard no more. It is a tale
Told by an idiot, full of sound and fury
Signifying nothing.   *Macbeth* V · 5

O that this too too solid flesh would melt,
Thaw and resolve itself into a dew,
Or that the Everlasting had not fixed
His canon 'gainst self-slaughter. O God, God,
How weary, stale, flat, and unprofitable
Seem to me all the uses of this world!
Fie on't, ah fie, 'tis an unweeded garden
That grows to seed, things rank and gross in
    nature
Possess it merely. That it should come to this —
But two months dead, nay not so much, not
    two —
So excellent a King, that was to this
Hyperion to a satyr, so loving to my mother,
That he might not beteem the winds of heaven
Visit her face too roughly. Heaven and earth,
Must I remember? Why she would hang on him
As if increase of appetite had grown
By what it fed on, and yet within a month —
Let me not think on't — frailty, thy name is
    woman.
A little month or e'er those shoes were old
With which she followed my poor father's body,
Like Niobe all tears, why she, even she —
O God, a beast that wants discourse of reason

Would have mourned longer — married with my
    uncle,
My father's brother, but no more like my father
Than I to Hercules — within a month;
Ere yet the salt of most unrighteous tears
Had left the flushing in her gallèd eyes,
She married — o most wicked speed, to post
With such dexterity to incestuous sheets.
It is not, nor it cannot come to good,
But break, my heart, for I must hold my tongue.

Hamlet I · 2

POLONIUS:

Yet here Laertes? Aboard, aboard, for shame;
The wind sits in the shoulder of your sail,
And you are stayed for. There — my blessing
    with thee.
And these few precepts in thy memory
Look thou character. Give thy thoughts no
    tongue,
Nor any unproportioned thought his act.
Be thou familiar, but by no means vulgar.
Those friends thou hast, and their adoption tried,
Grapple them unto thy soul with hoops of steel;
But do not dull thy palm with entertainment

43

Of each new-hatched, unfledged courage.
    Beware
Of entrance to a quarrel, but being in,
Bear't that th' opposed may beware of thee.
Give every man thy ear, but few thy voice;
Take each man's censure, but reserve thy
    judgement.
Costly thy habit as thy purse can buy,
But not expressed in fancy; rich, not gaudy,
For the apparel oft proclaims the man;
And they in France of the best rank and station,
Or of the most select and generous, chief in that.
Neither a borrower nor a lender be,
For loan oft loses both itself and friend,
And borrowing dulleth edge of husbandry.
This above all, to thine own self be true,
And it must follow, as the night the day,
Thou canst not then be false to any man.

Hamlet I · 3

HAMLET:

O what a rogue and peasant slave am I!
Is it not monstrous that this player here
But in a fiction, in a dream of passion,
Could force his soul so to his own conceit,
That from her working all his visage wanned;

44

Tears in his eyes, distraction in his aspect,
A broken voice, and his whole function suiting
With forms to his conceit — and all for nothing?
For Hecuba!
What's Hecuba to him, or he to Hecuba,
That he should weep for her? What would he do,
Had he the motive and the cue for passion
That I have? He would drown the stage with
        tears,
And cleave the general ear with horrid speech,
Make mad the guilty, and appal the free,
Confound the ignorant, and amaze indeed
The very faculties of eyes and ears; yet I,
A dull and muddy-mettled rascal, peak
Like John-a-dreams, unpregnant of my cause,
And can say nothing; no, not for a King,
Upon whose property and most dear life
A damned defeat was made. Am I a coward?
Who calls me villain, breaks my pate across,
Plucks off my beard, and blows it in my face,
Tweaks me by the nose, gives me the lie i' th'
        throat,
As deep as to the lungs — who does me this ha?
'Swounds, I should take it; for it cannot be
But I am pigeon-livered, and lack gall
To make oppression bitter, or ere this

I should ha' fatted all the region kites
With this slave's offal. Bloody, bawdy villain,
Remorseless, treacherous, lecherous, kindless
　　villain!
O vengeance!
Why, what an ass am I. This is most brave,
That I, the son of a dear father murdered,
Prompted to my revenge by heaven and hell,
Must like a whore unpack my heart with words,
And fall a-cursing like a very drab,
A scullion!

Hamlet II · 2

CLAUDIUS:

O my offence is rank, it smells to heaven;
It hath the primal eldest curse upon't,
A brother's murder. Pray can I not,
Though inclination be as sharp as will.
My stronger guilt defeats my strong intent,
And like a man to double business bound,
I stand in pause where I shall first begin,
And both neglect. What if this cursèd hand
Were thicker than itself with brother's blood,
Is there not rain enough in the sweet heavens
To wash it white as snow? Whereto serves mercy
But to confront the visage of offence?

And what's in prayer but this twofold force,
To be forstallèd ere we come to fall,
Or pardoned being down? Then I'll look up;
My fault is past. But o what form of prayer
Can serve my turn? Forgive me my foul murder?
That cannot be since I am still possessed
Of those effects for which I did the murder,
My crown, mine own ambition, and my Queen.
May one be pardoned and retain th' offence?
In the corrupted currents of this world,
Offence's gilded hand may shove by justice,
And oft 'tis seen the wicked prize itself
Buys out the law. But 'tis not so above;
There is no shuffling, there the action lies
In his true nature, and we ourselves compelled
Even to the teeth and forehead of our faults
To give in evidence. What then? What rests?
Try what repentance can — what can it not?
Yet what can it, when one cannot repent?
O wretched state, o bosom black as death,
O limèd soul, that struggling to be free,
Art more engaged! Help angels make assay.
Bow stubborn knees, and heart with strings of steel,
Be soft as sinews of the new-born babe.
All may be well.

Hamlet III · 3

To be, or not to be, that is the question —
Whether 'tis nobler in the mind to suffer
The slings and arrows of outrageous fortune,
Or to take arms against a sea of troubles,
And by opposing end them. To die, to sleep —
No more; and by a sleep to say we end
The heart-ache, and the thousand natural shocks
That flesh is heir to; 'tis a consumption
Devoutly to be wished. To die, to sleep —
To sleep, perchance to dream, ay there's the rub,
For in that sleep of death what dreams may come
When we have shuffled off this mortal coil,
Must give us pause; there's the respect
That makes calamity of so long life.
For who would bear the whips and scorns of
        time,
Th' oppressor's wrong, the proud man's
        contumely,
The pangs of despisèd love, the law's delay,
The insolence of office, and the spurns
That patient merit of th' unworthy takes,
When he himself might his quietus make
With a bare bodkin? Who would fardels bear,
To grunt and sweat under a weary life,
But that the dread of something after death,

The undiscovered country, from whose bourn
No traveller returns, puzzles the will,
And makes us rather bear those ills we have,
Than fly to others that we know not of?
Thus conscience does make cowards of us all,
And thus the native hue of resolution
Is sicklied o'er with the pale cast of thought,
And enterprises of great pitch and moment
With this regard their currents turn awry,
And lose the name of action.

Hamlet III · 1

HAMLET:

I am dead, Horatio. Wretched Queen, adieu.
You that look pale, and tremble at this chance,
That are but mutes or audience to this act,
Had I but time, as this fell sergeant Death
Is strict in his arrest, o I could tell you —
But let it be. Horatio, I am dead,
Thou livest; report me and my cause aright
To the unsatisfied.

· · ·

If thou didst ever hold me in thy heart,
Absent thee from felicity awhile,
And in this harsh world draw thy breath in pain,
To tell my story.

Hamlet V · 2

50

LEAR:

Blow winds, and crack your cheeks. Rage, blow,
You cataracts, and hurricanes, spout
Till you have drenched our steeples, drowned
    the cocks.
You sulphurous and thought-executing fires,
Vaunt-couriers of oak-cleaving thunderbolts,
Singe my white head. And thou all-shaking
    thunder,
Strike flat the thick rotundity o' th' world,
Crack nature's moulds, all germens spill at once,
That makes ingrateful man.

         • • •

Rumble thy bellyful. Spit fire, spout rain.
Nor rain, wind, thunder, fire, are my daughters;
I tax not you, you elements, with unkindness.
I never gave you kingdom, called you children;
You owe me no subscription. Then let fall
Your horrible pleasure. Here I stand your slave,
A poor, infirm, weak, and despised old man.
But yet I call you servile ministers,
That will with two pernicious daughters join
Your high-engendered battles 'gainst a head
So old and white as this. O! O 'tis foul.

King Lear III · 2

OTHELLO:

It is the cause, it is the cause, my soul —
Let me not name it to you, you chaste stars —
It is the cause. Yet I'll not shed her blood,
Nor scar that whiter skin of hers than snow,
And smooth as monumental alabaster.
Yet she must die, else she'll betray more men.
Put out the light, and then put out the light.
If I quench thee, thou flaming minister,
I can again thy former light restore,
Should I repent me. But once put out thy light,
Thou cunning'st pattern of excelling nature,
I know not where is that Promethean heat
That can thy light relume. When I have plucked
     thy rose,
I cannot give it vital growth again,
It needs must wither. I'll smell thee on the tree.
     [*Kisses her*]
O balmy breath, that dost almost persuade
Justice to break her sword. One more, one more.
Be thus when thou art dead, and I will kill thee,
And love thee after. One more, and that's the last.
So sweet, was ne'er so fatal. I must weep,
But they are cruel tears. This sorrow's heavenly,
It strikes where it doth love.

Othello V · 2

OTHELLO:

> Behold, I have a weapon;
> A better never did itself sustain
> Upon a soldier's thigh. I have seen the day
> That with this little arm, and this good sword,
> I have made my way through more impediments
> Than twenty times your stop. But o vain boast,
> Who can control his fate? 'Tis not so now.
> Be not afraid, though you do see me weaponed.
> Here is my journey's end, here is my butt,
> And very sea-mark of my utmost sail.
> Do you go back dismayed? 'Tis a lost fear;
> Man but a rush against Othello's breast,
> And he retires. Where should Othello go?
> Now; how dost thou look now? O ill-starred
>   wench,
> Pale as thy smock. When we shall meet at compt,
> This look of thine will hurl my soul from heaven,
> And fiends will snatch at it. Cold, cold, my girl —
> Even like thy chastity.
> O cursèd, cursèd slave! Whip me ye devils,
> From the possession of this heavenly sight.
> Blow me about in winds. Roast me in sulphur.
> Wash me in steep-down gulfs of liquid fire.
> O Desdemona! Desdemona! Dead!

Othello V · 2

Soft you; a word or two before you go.
I have done the state some service, and they
    know't.
No more of that. I pray you in your letters,
When you shall these unlucky deeds relate,
Speak of me, as I am. Nothing extenuate,
Nor set down aught in malice. Then must you
    speak
Of one that loved not wisely, but too well;
Of one not easily jealous, but being wrought,
Perplexed in the extreme; of one whose hand,
Like the base Indian, threw a pearl away,
Richer than all his tribe; of one whose subdued
    eyes,
Albeit unusèd to the melting mood,
Drops tears as fast as the Arabian trees
Their medicinable gum. Set you down this;
And say besides, that in Aleppo once,
Where a malignant and a turbaned Turk
Beat a Venetian, and traduced the state,
I took by th' throat the circumcisèd dog,
And smote him — thus.

    [*Stabs himself*]

                    Othello V · 2

ANTONY:

Unarm, Eros, the long day's task is done,
And we must sleep.

          •   •   •

                                    Off, pluck off.
The seven-fold shield of Ajax cannot keep
The battery from my heart. O cleave, my sides!
Heart, once be stronger than thy continent,
Crack thy frail case! Apace Eros, apace.
No more a soldier. Bruisèd pieces, go,
You have been nobly borne. From me awhile.
    [*Exit* EROS]
I will o'ertake thee Cleopatra, and
Weep for my pardon. So it must be, for now
All length is torture. Since the torch is out,
Lie down, and stray no farther. Now all labour
Mars what it does; yea, very force entangles
Itself with strength. Seal then, and all is done.
Eros! I come, my Queen. Eros! Stay for me.
Where souls do couch on flowers, we'll hand in
    hand,
And with our sprightly port make the ghosts
    gaze.
Dido and her Æneas shall want troops,
And all the haunt be ours. Come Eros, Eros!

                  Antony and Cleopatra IV · 14

ANTONY:

I am dying, Egypt, dying; only
I here importune death awhile, until
Of many thousand kisses the poor last
I lay upon thy lips.

           •   •   •

CLEOPATRA:

               Noblest of men, woo't die?
Hast thou no care of me? Shall I abide
In this dull world, which in thy absence is
No better than a sty? O see, my women,
   [ANTONY *dies*]
The crown o' th' earth does melt. My lord!
O withered is the garland of the war,
The soldiers' pole is fall'n: young boys and girls
Are level now with men; the odds is gone,
And there is nothing left remarkable
Beneath the visiting moon.

       Antony and Cleopatra IV · 15

CLEOPATRA:

Give me my robe, put on my crown, I have
Immortal longings in me. Now no more
The juice of Egypt's grape shall moist this lip.
Yare, yare, good Iras; quick. Methinks I hear
Antony call; I see him rouse himself

To praise my noble act. I hear him mock
The luck of Cæsar, which the gods give men
To excuse their after wrath. Husband, I come.
Now to that name my courage prove my title.
I am fire and air; my other elements
I give to baser life. So, have you done?
Come then, and take the last warmth of my lips.
Farewell kind Charmian — Iras, long farewell.

    [*Kisses them.* IRAS *falls and dies*]
Have I the aspic in my lips? Dost fall?
If thou and nature can so gently part,
The stroke of death is as a lover's pinch,
Which hurts, and is desired. Dost thou lie still?
If thus thou vanishèd, thou tell'st the world
It is not worth leave-taking.

              •   •   •

                  This proves me base.
If she first meet the curlèd Antony,
He'll make demand of her, and spend that kiss
Which is my heaven to have. Come thou mortal
    wretch,   [*Applies an asp to her breast*]
With thy sharp teeth this knot intrinsicate
Of life at once untie. Poor venomous fool,
Be angry, and dispatch. O couldst thou speak,
That I might hear thee call great Cæsar ass,
Unpolicied.   *Antony and Cleopatra* V · 2

KATHARINE:

A woman moved, is like a fountain troubled,
Muddy, ill-seeming, thick, bereft of beauty,
And while it is so, none so dry or thirsty
Will deign to sip, or touch one drop of it.
Thy husband is thy lord, thy life, thy keeper,
Thy head, thy sovereign; one that cares for thee,
And for thy maintenance; commits his body
To painful labour both by sea and land;
To watch the night in storms, the day in cold,
Whilst thou liest warm at home, secure and safe;
And craves no other tribute at thy hands
But love, fair looks, and true obedience —
Too little payment for so great a debt.
Such duty as the subject owes the prince,
Even such a woman oweth to her husband;
And when she is froward, peevish, sullen, sour,
And not obedient to his honest will,
What is she but a foul contending rebel,
And graceless traitor to her loving lord?
I am ashamed that women are so simple
To offer war, where they should kneel for peace;
Or seek for rule, supremacy, and sway,
When they are bound to serve, love, and obey.
Why are our bodies soft, and weak, and smooth,
Unapt to toil and trouble in the world,

But that our soft conditions, and our hearts,
Should well agree with our external parts?
Come, come, you froward and unable worms,
My mind hath been as big as one of yours,
My heart as great, my reason haply more,
To bandy word for word, and frown for frown.
But now I see our lances are but straws;
Our strength as weak, our weakness past
     compare,
That seeming to be most, which we indeed least
     are.

            The Taming of the Shrew V · 2

PROSPERO:

Our revels now are ended. These our actors,
As I foretold you, were all spirits, and
Are melted into air, into thin air,
And like the baseless fabric of this vision
The cloud-capped towers, the gorgeous palaces,
The solemn temples, the great globe itself,
Yea, all which it inherit, shall dissolve,
And like this insubstantial pageant faded
Leave not a rack behind. We are such stuff
As dreams are made on; and our little life
Is rounded with a sleep.

            The Tempest IV · 1